WHEELS
AND AXLES

Erinn Banting

MEDIA ENHANCED BOOKS

AV2
BY WEIGL™

ADDED VALUE • AUDIO VISUAL

www.av2books.com

AV² provides enriched content that supplements and complements this book. Weigl's AV² books strive to create inspired learning and engage young minds in a total learning experience.

Your AV² Media Enhanced books come alive with...

Audio
Listen to sections of the book read aloud.

Key Words
Study vocabulary, and complete a matching word activity.

Go to **www.av2books.com**, and enter this book's unique code.

Video
Watch informative video clips.

Quizzes
Test your knowledge.

BOOK CODE

K889710

Embedded Weblinks
Gain additional information for research.

Slide Show
View images and captions, and prepare a presentation.

AV² by Weigl brings you media enhanced books that support active learning.

Try This!
Complete activities and hands-on experiments.

... and much, much more!

Published by AV² by Weigl
350 5th Avenue, 59th Floor
New York, NY 10118

Website: www.av2books.com   www.weigl.com

Library of Congress Cataloging-in-Publication Data

Banting, Erinn.
Wheels and axles / Erinn Banting.
  p. cm. -- (Simple machines)
 Summary: "Presents information on simple machines with a focus on wheels and axles. Explains what wheels and axles are, how wheels and axles work, and includes examples of past and present uses. Intended for third to fifth grade students"--Provided by publisher.
Includes index.
ISBN 978-1-62127-429-2 (hardcover : alk. paper) -- ISBN 978-1-62127-435-3 (softcover : alk. paper)
1. Wheels--Juvenile literature. 2. Axles--Juvenile literature. I. Title.
TJ181.5.B36 2013
621.8'2--dc23
                2012041028

Printed in the United States of America in North Mankato, Minnesota
1 2 3 4 5 6 7 8 9 0 17 16 15 14 13

042013
WEP040413

Project Coordinator: Alexis Roumanis
Design: Mandy Christiansen

Photo Credits
Weigl acknowledges Getty Images as the primary photo supplier for this title. Page 18, Alamy. Page 22, A. R. Roumanis.

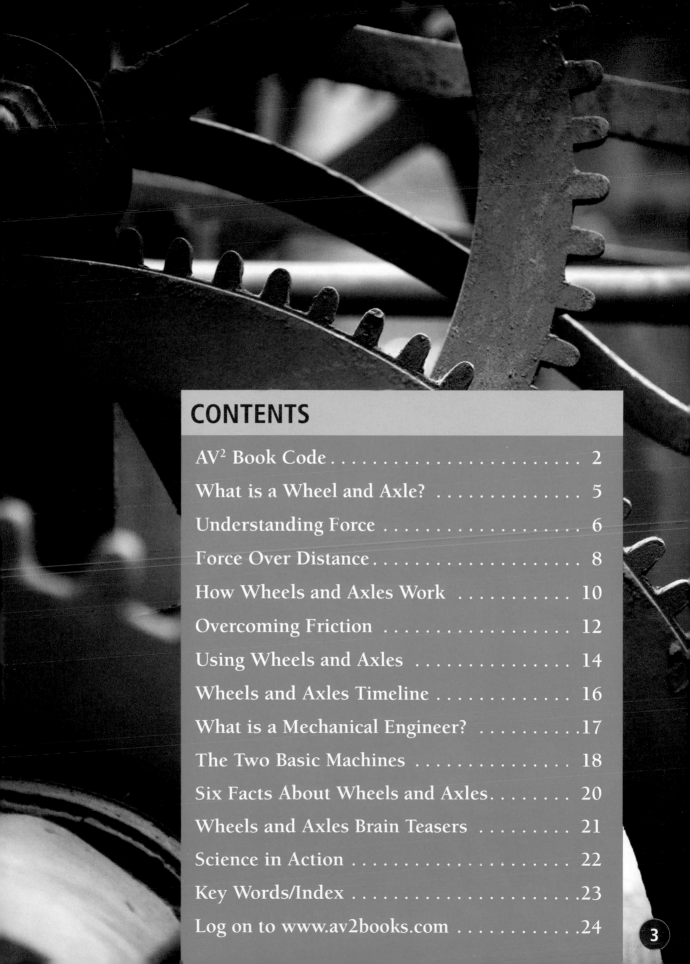

CONTENTS

People use skateboards for transportation, as well as for sport. Skateboards have special rubber wheels that allow the rider to roll over objects, such as small rocks or twigs. This helps reduce accidents. Many skateboarders can perform amazing tricks with their skateboards.

What is a Wheel and Axle?

A wheel is a circle-shaped object that rotates around its center. Wheels often have an axle in the middle to hold them in place while they rotate. Wheels and axles were invented thousands of years ago, but they are still used in a wide range of machines.

The wheel and axle is a simple machine. There are six simple machines. They are the inclined plane, the lever, the pulley, the screw, the wedge, and the wheel and axle. All simple machines make work easier. They do not have batteries or motors. They do not add any **energy** of their own to help people do work. Instead, simple machines work by changing the **effort** needed to move an object.

■ Airplanes use retractable wheels called landing gear for takeoff and landing.

Understanding Force

Force is a push or a pull that causes an object to move or change its direction. When an object is not moving, or at rest, all of the forces pushing or pulling it are balanced. This balance is called **equilibrium**.

When scientists study forces and how objects move, there are three measurements they need to know. They must know the object's **weight**, how fast it is moving, and the amount of force that is causing the object to move. Understanding forces, how forces affect objects, and how objects affect each other can make it easier to move objects.

■ Tennis players create a great deal of force when they strike the ball. Some professional tennis players can hit the ball more than 150 miles (241 kilometers) per hour.

What is Gravity?

Gravity is a force that pulls one object toward another. All objects have some gravity, though it is often very weak. An object's gravity is related to its **mass**. The more mass an object has, the greater its force of gravity and the pull it creates. Earth is a massive object, which means it has a strong gravity. This gravity pulls other objects toward the center of Earth.

Earth's gravity gives weight to an object's mass. A large rock has a great deal of mass. Earth's gravity pulls on this mass to create a heavy weight. A heavy weight needs a great force to make it move. This is why moving large objects often takes a great deal of effort.

MASS VS. WEIGHT

People often think mass and weight are the same, but they are very different. Mass is how much material an object contains. Weight is how strongly gravity pulls on an object. Mass is usually measured in kilograms, while weight is often measured in pounds.

A person with a mass of 91 kilograms weighs 200 pounds, but this is only true on Earth. This is because Earth's gravity pulls on a 91-kg mass with a force of 200 pounds. The Moon's much weaker gravity would only pull on a 91-kg mass with a force of 33 pounds. Also, if the person were to leave Earth on a space shuttle, he or she would become weightless. Even though the person would then weigh 0 pounds, his or her mass of 91 kg would not change.

Force Over Distance

In science, **work** happens when a force is used to move an object over a distance. For work to happen, the force must be applied in the same direction the object is moving.

In other words, lifting a rock off the ground is work because the force applied to pull the rock up is going in the same upward direction that the rock is moving. On the other hand, holding a rock while walking is not work. This is because the forward movement of walking is not related to the upward force that is holding the rock up.

■ Moving extremely heavy objects takes a great deal of force. Dump trucks use very large wheels to help transfer the force created by the vehicle's motor into forward motion.

As the force needed to move an object increases, the work involved in moving it also increases. This also applies to distance. The amount of work needed to move the object increases as the distance the object must move increases.

Simple machines make doing work easier. They do this by changing the amount and the direction of the force needed to move the object. Though less force is needed, simple machines require moving a greater distance.

DOING WORK

One way a wheel and axle does work is to help move objects. The wheel makes work easier by reducing the amount of surface that is touching the ground. Think about how much work it would take to move a ball compared to moving a block. The ball will be easier to move because less of its surface touches the ground at any one time.

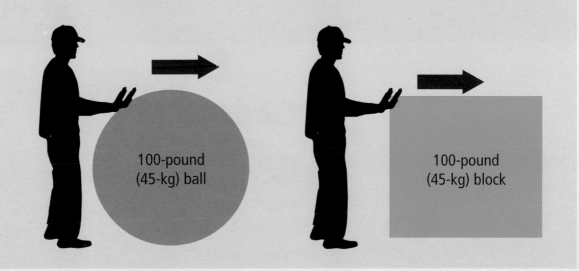

100-pound (45-kg) ball

100-pound (45-kg) block

How Wheels and Axles Work

The wheel and axle make work easier because it offers a **mechanical advantage**. This means that it takes less force to move an object with a wheel and axle than it would without using a wheel and axle.

One way the wheel and axle works is to act as a kind of lever. A wheel and axle is a lever that can move in a complete circle. As the wheel turns, the axle attached to it turns as well. The mechanical advantage is created because the small axle spins with a greater force than the larger wheel to which it is attached. When a wheel turns with a small force, the axle turns with a greater force.

■ A race car engine turns the axle, creating enough force to spin the wheel and push the car forward.

The greater the distance a wheel travels to complete one turn, the more force it transfers to the axle. In other words, as the size of the wheel increases, the force transferred to the axle increases as well. This means less force may be applied to the wheel in order to move the axle. Doorknobs work in this way. The small force applied to turning the doorknob is magnified in the small axle that allows the door to open.

As with all simple machines, there is a trade-off between distance and force. A larger wheel transfers more force to the axle, but it must travel a greater distance with each turn.

CALCULATING EFFORT

To determine the mechanical advantage of a wheel and axle, divide the **radius** of the wheel by the radius of the axle. The radius of the wheel, 24 inches, is divided by the radius of the axle, 2 inches. 24 divided by 2 is 12. This means that the force used to turn the 24-inch wheel will be multiplied 12 times on the axle.

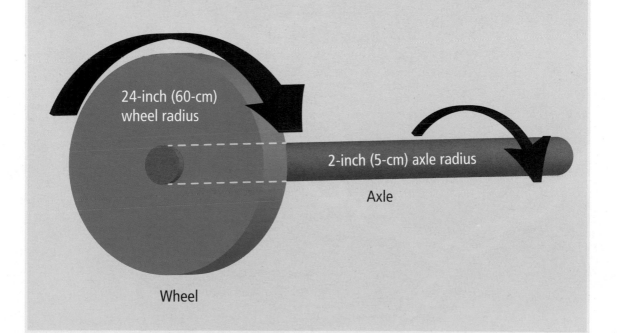

24-inch (60-cm) wheel radius

2-inch (5-cm) axle radius

Axle

Wheel

Overcoming Friction

Friction is a force that is created when two surfaces come in contact with each other. A large amount of friction makes a strong grip between two surfaces. This can make it difficult to slide one object over the surface of another. Wheels create friction when they come in contact with a surface.

Friction also affects how much work is needed to move objects. Dragging a heavy object along the ground may take a great deal of work. This is because of the friction the dragging would create. A wheel and axle could move the same object with less work. Wheels create a small amount of friction because only a small part of the wheel touches the ground.

■ Sometimes, a car's tires may not create enough friction to drive on very icy roads. In this case, drivers use chains that dig into the ice to create the friction needed to move the car forward.

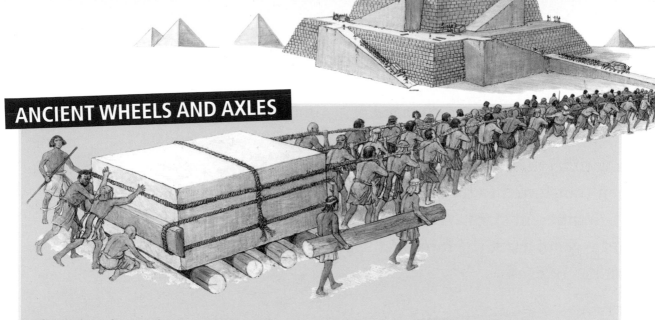

ANCIENT WHEELS AND AXLES

The earliest forms of transportation did not have axles or wheels. This made moving people or heavy **loads** from place to place very difficult. Goods or building materials had to be carried or dragged along the ground.

When wheels were invented, moving heavy objects from place to place became much easier. Early humans realized that, to move things more easily, they needed to reduce friction. Wheels reduce friction, so objects sitting on wheels can be moved the same distance with much less force.

Rollers were made by placing a number of logs on the ground side by side. The material being transported was laid on top of the logs. When the load was pulled, the logs rolled, and the load moved forward. According to some **archaeologists**, the shift from rollers to wooden wheels happened as early as 8000 BC.

Using Wheels and Axles

Wheels and axles have changed over time. A gear is a type of wheel with teeth around the edge. The teeth on the gears fit with teeth on other gears. Forces applied to one gear are then transferred to the other gears. Gears are most useful when different sizes are combined. Depending on the size of the gears used, the force and speed of the turning gears can be changed.

Large gears are easy to turn, but they need to be turned very quickly to push an object, such as a car or a bike, forward. Smaller gears need more force to turn, but they can move an object forward faster.

■ Spokes are rods that connect the center of a wheel to the edge, or rim. They are often on bicycles because spoked wheels are much lighter than solid wheels.

Wheels and Axles in Action

Wheels and axles are found in many common machines.

CARS AND TRUCKS

Cars use wheels and axles. Instead of turning the wheel to power the axle, the car's engine turns the axle, which then turns the wheel and moves the car.

WATCHES

Some watches use gears to keep time. As a coiled spring unwinds, its power is transferred to a series of gears. These gears then move the hands on the watch.

MUSIC AND MOVIES

An axle holds the disc in place inside a DVD or CD player. The axle spins the disc so the machine can read it.

TRAINS

Some trains have straight axles. A straight axle connects to a wheel on each side of the train. With this type of axle, moving one wheel also moves the other wheel the same distance.

Wheels and Axles Timeline

2000 BC 680 BC 50 BC 1500 AD 1550 1600 1650 1700 1750 1800 1850 1900 1950 2000

1 2 3 4 5 6 7 8 9 10

1 2000 BC
Wheeled chariots are used in the Middle East.

2 680 BC
Chariot racing is added to the ancient Greek Olympic Games.

3 50 BC
Julius Caesar builds a racetrack for chariots in the city of Rome.

4 1478 AD
Leonardo da Vinci designs a car-like vehicle.

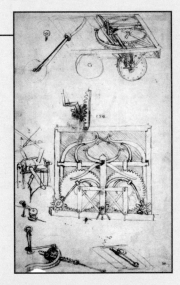

5 1817
The bicycle is invented.

6 1885
In Germany, Karl Benz invents what many consider to be the first automobile.

7 1903
Henry Ford starts the Ford Motor Company.

8 1971
Astronauts on the Moon use the "moon buggy," a vehicle designed for space.

9 2002
A 5,100 year old wheel is discovered by scientists in Europe.

10 2010
The number of cars in the world passes 1 billion.

What is a Mechanical Engineer?

Mechanical **engineers** design and build a wide variety of objects, from roller coasters to robots. To learn all they need to know, mechanical engineers must go to school for many years. They must be very good at math and science. Engineers must be creative and love solving problems. They also enjoy working with others, since many of the projects they work on can be very large and complex. Sometimes, they will need to invent tools to help them solve a problem. Mechanical engineers are needed in almost every kind of industry.

Leslie Livesay

Leslie Livesay is an American engineer. When she was a child, Leslie learned that the *Voyager* spacecraft had passed the planet Saturn. Leslie became interested in space and other planets. At university, Leslie studied math and electrical engineering. After school, she started working with NASA. She helped design the Mars *Pathfinder* rover. In 1997, this robotic vehicle landed on Mars to study the planet's surface and **atmosphere**.

■ On August 6, 2012, the *Curiosity* rover landed on Mars. This rover was designed at NASA by many different engineers, including mechanical engineers. *Curiosity's* mission is to study the Martian climate and search for evidence of past life on Mars.

The Two Basic Machines

The inclined plane and the lever are the most basic of all simple machines. In fact, all six simple machines can be seen as one of these two most basic machines.

TYPES OF INCLINED PLANE

The inclined plane is the simplest of the simple machines. Any slope, such as a hill, is an inclined plane.

A wedge is two inclined planes put together.

A screw is an inclined plane wrapped around a center bar.

TYPES OF LEVERS

A lever is a bar that rests on a pivot, or **fulcrum**. Pushing down on one end of the bar helps to lift a load on the other end of the bar.

A wheel and axle is a lever in which the bar circles around the fulcrum, or axle.

A pulley is a lever that uses a wheel for a fulcrum and a rope instead of a bar.

Complex Machines

Simple machines can be combined to make other kinds of machines. When two simple machines are combined, this new machine is often called a compound or complex machine. Wheels and axles are found in many common machines.

PULLEY

A wheel and axle can be found on many types of pulleys. The pulley itself is usually attached to another object with the help of screws.

LEVER

A lever is a movable bar that rests on a solid point called the fulcrum.

JET ENGINE

Jet engines use wheels and axles to create the force needed to keep jet planes in the air. Some experimental jets have flown more than 6,800 miles (10,900 km) per hour.

Six Facts About Wheels and Axles

A hand-crank eggbeater uses a gear wheel to spin the axle of the beater. The beater is also a type of wheel.

Most cars and trucks use a split axle. With this type of axle, the wheels on each side are attached to a different shaft. This allows each wheel to spin at different speeds.

Globes spin on an axle.

The Laxey Wheel on the Isle of Man is the largest working water wheel in the world. Water wheels help change flowing water into electricity.

A circular saw uses an axle to spin a jagged wheel.

Paddle wheels are used by steamships. A steam engine creates the energy that spins the wheel, moving the boat forward.

Wheels and Axles
Brain Teasers

1 What is a wheel?

2 What is an axle?

3 How is friction created?

4 What are spokes?

5 How many types of simple machines are there?

6 What is a gear?

7 What powers the gears in some watches?

8 When did Henry Ford start the Ford Motor Company?

9 When were the first wooden wheels made?

10 How is work defined?

ANSWERS: 1. A wheel is a circle-shaped object that rotates around its center 2. An axle is a straight rod connected to the center of the wheel 3. Friction is created when one surface rubs against another 4. Spokes are rods that connect the center of a wheel to the edge, or rim 5. There are six types of simple machines. 6. A gear is a wheel with teeth around the edge 7. A coiled spring 8. 1903 9. Wooden wheels were developed as early as 8000 BC 10. Force applied over distance to move an object

Science in Action

Roll With It

Design your own car by building a simple machine.

Materials Needed

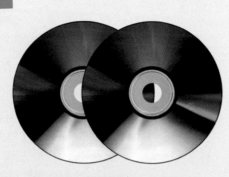

two blank CDs or DVDs

marker

Directions

1 With the help of an adult, find two blank CDs.

2 Find a marker that will fit into the holes in the center of the CDs.

3 Place the CDs on either end of the marker. You may need to remove the cap from the marker for the CD to fit in the marker.

4 Roll your axle and wheels across the table or floor.

Key Words

archaeologists: scientists who study the remains of old cultures

atmosphere: the body of gases that surrounds Earth

effort: the force being used to move a load

energy: power needed to do work

engineers: people who use science to solve practical problems

equilibrium: a state when all the forces acting on an object are balanced

friction: the force caused by two surfaces coming in contact with one another

fulcrum: the point where a lever turns

loads: the objects or substances being worked on by a simple machine

mass: a measure of the amount of matter an object contains

mechanical advantage: a measure of how much easier a task is made when a simple machine is used

radius: the distance from the center to the outside edge of a circle

weight: the force of gravity's pull on an object's mass

work: force applied over distance to move an object

Index

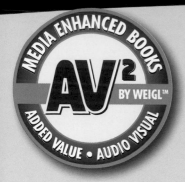

Log on to www.av2books.com

AV² by Weigl brings you media enhanced books that support active learning. Go to www.av2books.com, and enter the special code found on page 2 of this book. You will gain access to enriched and enhanced content that supplements and complements this book. Content includes video, audio, weblinks, quizzes, a slide show, and activities.

AV² Online Navigation

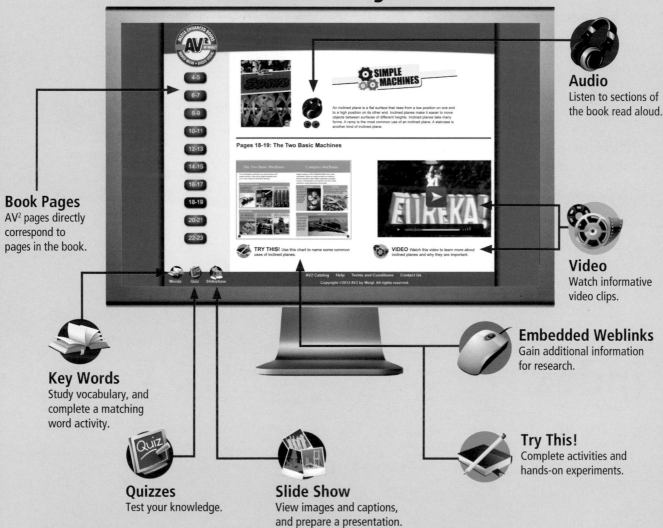

Book Pages
AV² pages directly correspond to pages in the book.

Audio
Listen to sections of the book read aloud.

Video
Watch informative video clips.

Embedded Weblinks
Gain additional information for research.

Key Words
Study vocabulary, and complete a matching word activity.

Try This!
Complete activities and hands-on experiments.

Quizzes
Test your knowledge.

Slide Show
View images and captions, and prepare a presentation.

AV² was built to bridge the gap between print and digital. We encourage you to tell us what you like and what you want to see in the future.

Sign up to be an AV² Ambassador at www.av2books.com/ambassador.